Journey to JESUS

ALLEN BOURGEOIS

ISBN 978-1-68570-679-1 (paperback)
ISBN 978-1-68570-680-7 (digital)

Copyright © 2023 by Allen Bourgeois

All rights reserved. No part of this publication may be reproduced, distributed, or transmitted in any form or by any means, including photocopying, recording, or other electronic or mechanical methods without the prior written permission of the publisher. For permission requests, solicit the publisher via the address below.

Christian Faith Publishing
832 Park Avenue
Meadville, PA 16335
www.christianfaithpublishing.com

Printed in the United States of America

Growing up in a small country town in Southeast Louisiana in the 1940s and 1950s was not easy, because of the economy and low wages. Having a garden and farm animals helped a lot. My parents never owned a car, so I got plenty of sunshine and exercise.

Things changed in my late teens and early twenties. I became depressed and anxious, had low self-esteem, ate a poor diet, and made bad decisions. My doctor said I could die of a stroke or heart attack at any time. He wanted to see me every ten days. As the weeks went by, I changed my diet and noticed my health gradually improving. I felt better about myself and made better decisions. I got a better job, and my health continued to improve. I learned to play the guitar and write songs.

Then God gave me a dream. In the dream I entered the cargo section of an eighteen-wheeler and saw thousands of books waist-high all the way to the front. Most of the books were evil or worldly. I climbed to the middle section, reached down and saw a Bible, and pulled it out of the pile. I bought a Bible and began to read and study it every day.

I sat at my desk for hours and attempted to write my first Christian song. I had no title or words, so I said, "I can't do this." When I got to the door to get ready for bed, everything changed. A voice told me to go back and sit down. Then I was told to pick up my pen and write. I knew then it could only be God. When I got to the last line of the song, I was told to pick up my guitar. As soon as I touched it, the entire melody came to me, and I began playing it and singing the song God gave me: "Do It All for Jesus." I then fell to my knees and repented for everything I had ever done to offend Him.

Later on I went to a music school in New Orleans. I was invited to a spirit-filled church on the west bank in Marrero, Louisiana, where God filled me with His spirit after about three months of continuous daily prayer. After a Sunday morning service in July of 1981, I went to the restroom and stopped, thinking why I hadn't received God's spirit after praying so much. I opened my Bible to Joshua 1:9, and it said, "Have I not commanded thee? Be strong and of a good courage; be not afraid, neither be thou dismayed: for the Lord thy God is with thee whithersoever thou goest." At that moment I felt His spirit enter my body from the top of my head to the soles of my feet. I was speaking in a language I had never spoken in before, but it was very clear and pronounced. After I came out of the spirit, I drove over the Greater New Orleans Bridge and headed to a cafeteria for lunch. There were about three hundred people there of all cultural backgrounds and walks of life. When I looked at everyone, it was like I had known them all my life. I prayed for every single person whom I looked at. The spirit of God was on me so strongly that they could have spit in my face or slapped me in the face and I still could've looked at them and with the kindest tone possible told them how much Jesus loved them. I was looking at them through the eyes of Jesus.

I stayed that way for months, even on my job. People I worked with even noticed a change for the better in me. I thank Him for He has blessed me abundantly since then on my journey to Jesus. I give Him all the glory, praise, and honor for the songs and testimonies He has given me since that day in July 1981 and then all throughout the years since then. It is a privilege and honor to be able to live a life that pleases Him!

It was a forty-five-mile drive one way to that church and forty-five miles back home. I went there for ten months and began looking for a spirit-filled church closer to my home. I prayed about it, and God sent me to a church in Gonzales, Louisiana. My health and finances continued to improve. I was greatly blessed to be a part of that church. The pastor was a great teacher of God's Word. Since then God has blessed me with many great new songs that have blessed and encouraged people. The type and style of Bible-based Christian songs that I write encourage and inspire others in the ways of the Lord. God has blessed me with a song ministry called "Songs for Jesus." I have sung these songs for about twenty-five years across Southeast and Southwest Louisiana. The very first Christian song God has ever blessed me with is called "Do It All for Jesus." It changed my life forever. These are the words:

> Let the songs you sing bring happiness to others and the things you do follow them through with love. Set the time aside to guide you home to Jesus. Let His kindness find you when you need His love. Do it all for Jesus. Do it all for love. Let His kindness shine upon you, from above. Take a closer look at all of God's creation, to appreciate the beauty that He shares. Watch His love as it covers every nation, when in our heart we start to show we care. Do it all for Jesus. Do it all for love. Let His kindness shine upon you, from above. Let your love show like rainbows in the summer. Let your problems die like withered leaves in fall. Let the songs you sing bring joy to greater numbers. Let the harmony of happiness stand tall. Do it all for Jesus. Do it all for love. Let His kindness shine upon you, from above.

I have sung the following song many times and also use it as a personal prayer to God. This song is called "Forever You Reign" and is one of the songs God has blessed me with so I can bless others.

> God, You're the same today, as You were yesterday! Worthy of praise, in all of Your ways.
> Your mercy moves me to build the faith I have in You. Your kingdom remains. Forever You reign!
> You heal the lame; they walk. You feed the hungry still. Saving souls, Your great desire!

You make the lion roar, the eagle soar. God, You're a consuming fire! Jesus, I lift Your name higher! Your ways are supreme. Forever You reign! Creating stars above, calling them all by name. The heavens proclaim, "Forever You reign!" Doing miracles, here, there, everywhere! Answering prayers, showing You care! Supplying needs, my God! You never stop! You're living water flowing from the rock! Your spirit's rolling back the sea for me! I have liberty; I have victory! Oh, wonderful, powerful God! Forever You reign! Your ways never change! Everything I do is before Your eyes! You're the Great I Am! You are glorified! You're not in that grave; You're alive! Your kingdom remains! Forever You reign! Your kingdom remains! Forever You reign!

Another song God has blessed me with is one called "None like Jesus." These are the words:

> I can say with no regret I have never met no one like Jesus. There's none like Jesus. When I'm weary or depressed, I find peace and rest. I know that I am blessed. There is none like Jesus!
> I get my help from heaven, with God on the scene. I have victory! Liberty! Sunshine through the rain! That comes from Jesus! There's none like Jesus! No one like Jesus! Praise to His name! Praise to His name! He forgives me of my sins. There's no fault in Him! I have no better friend.
> There is none like Jesus. All His promises are true. I have healing through the name of Jesus.
> There is none like Jesus! I get my help from heaven, with God on the scene! I have victory! Liberty! Sunshine through the rain! That comes from Jesus! There's none like Jesus! No one like

> Jesus! Praise to His name! Praise to His name! I'll never need a plane to fly, or a train ride, to hurry to His side, to be blessed by Jesus. The many thoughts He has of me number more than sand. Part of a master plan, from none but Jesus! I get my help from heaven, with God on the scene. I have victory! Liberty! Sunshine through the rain! That comes from Jesus! There's none like Jesus! No one like Jesus! Praise to His name! Praise to His name!

At a church service one Sunday several years ago, to prove a point, the pastor asked someone to go to the wall and face it. He asked them what they saw. They said all they saw was the wall. Then he told them to step back a few steps and then tell him what they saw. They said that they saw a lot more than just the wall. That experience inspired me to write another song. I prayed about the song, and God blessed me with the title: "God's Always There for Me." This experience helped me realize that in order to get through our problems, sometimes we just need to step back and look at things from a different viewpoint. These are the words:

> The car won't start; it's in the shop. Bills are everywhere. The central air at home has stopped. It, too, will need repair. I put my face against the wall. Wall is all I see, till I step back and realize God's always there for me. God's always there for me, in the good times and the bad. A lantern at my feet, my anchor in the deep. Wherever I may be, God's always there for me. A different view will see me through problems every day. The phone may ring. A call could bring some things I dread to face. But God knows best in every test He allows to be. Oh, I have found that when I'm down, God's always there for me. God's always there for me, in the good times and the bad.

A lantern at my feet, my anchor in the deep.
Wherever I may be, God's always there for me.
Wherever I may be, God's always there for me.

While in prayer one day, I asked God to help me write a Christian song about gambling. And once again, God came through for me as He always does. A recording studio wanted $700 to record it, but I asked if they could go down to $500, and they agreed. I mentioned to a coworker how I did not have the money at the time to pay for it, and the very next day, she walked up to me and handed me the $500 I needed to record my song. God even provided me with the musicians and a really talented backup singer to sing with me at no additional cost. The title of my next song is "Salvation's No Game":

In a crowded casino, he's gambling his life, for fame and for riches, by the toss of the dice. All the money could buy him many friends and a name. But a soul needs Your touch, Lord. Salvation's no game. All that will matter when the cards are all faded and the last wheel has spun. When the gambling is over and no time remains. He'll be facing forever. Salvation's no game. There's a church in the county he passes and grins. He once heard a message: are you living in sin? He can still hear the preacher: does your life need a change? Let the Lord be your teacher. Salvation's no game. All that will matter when the cards are all faded and the last wheel has spun. When the gambling is over and no time remains. He'll be facing forever. Salvation's no game. On a big silver jet plane, he's bound for LA. From there to Las Vegas, then to Mexico way. Will a chance for the big time ever be worth the fame? Is it too late to learn, Lord, salvation's no game? All that will matter when the cards are all faded and the last wheel has spun. When the gambling is over and no time remains. He'll be facing forever. Salvation's no game. When the gambling is over and no time remains. He'll be facing forever. Salvation's no game.

Before I recorded that song, I attended a songwriters' meeting in Gonzales, Louisiana. There were about thirty-five other people from all over Louisiana in attendance. When the meeting was about to come to an end, right before that I asked the president of the Louisiana Songwriters Association if I could sing a song and they could critique it for me before the meeting dismissed, and she agreed. I sang the song acapella, and I looked straight ahead while I sang it. After I finished singing my song, they critiqued it for me and said they could not find anything that needed to change. Two men came up to me and asked, "Did you see everyone's expressions when you sang that song?" I told them I had not because I was looking straight at the wall. Then they said, "Well, we did. We're telling you that your song moved some people in this room." As people were leaving, I overheard several of them talking about that song. I pray about every single Christian song I write. God always helps me to write it, from beginning to end. I always pray that God helps me to get the point of each song across to the listener.

Before I got married, I took a vacation to Maine. I got stranded high up in the mountains in a rental car. I got stuck deep in sand as I tried to turn around and go back to New Hampshire to my motel. It was freezing cold with not a soul in sight for miles. I prayed as the sun began to set, "God, please help me get off this mountain!" About ten seconds later, a car pulled up to exactly where I was. And the driver went to the back of his car, pulled out a chain, hooked it to my rental car, and pulled me out. I wanted to pay him, but he didn't say a word. I took a closer look as he drove off, and there was no vehicle, just my rental car. I believe that God sent an angel in my time of need.

In my late thirties, I was driving on Highway 61 late at night heading back to Lutcher, Louisiana, where I lived. I had a rough day at work and was very tired. There was a swamp to my right and the

Blind River to my left. I asked God to please keep me awake, as it was very cold and windy that day. I couldn't keep my eyes open and fell asleep at the wheel. I was driving fifty-five miles per hour. I went off the road, ready to hit a concrete bridge in front of me in seconds. A voice screamed in my ear, "Wake up!" My head nearly hit the headliner, and I turned quickly back onto the road. I thanked God multiple times. I didn't fall asleep again until I got home.

I got married at forty-one years old, and my wife had four girls, ages two to eight years old. Finances got low after I changed jobs and paid for a place for us to live. We were at a church service, and I asked God to help me with finances. His answer was "Why do you keep asking Me for money? Go to your post office. It is there for you." My family and I went to the post office, and they all followed me inside. There was a check from the IRS for $750 that they overlooked and owed us.

A few years later, God sent me to a different church in Baton Rouge, Louisiana. A friend of my wife and me came down to visit us for a few days. Two of my wife's daughters came with us to this church along with our friend. I was praying and asked God which church He wanted us to go, and He told me which one to go to out of the five I had written down on a piece of paper. God told me to go to the church that was in the most crime-filled area in Baton Rouge, Louisiana. There were bars on the windows and doors of houses and businesses, and I had thought I made a mistake coming to this church. But when the pastor began preaching, I knew I had not made a mistake. My family and I were exactly where we were supposed to be. We got into the church, and we were waiting for the service to start, and then the pastor began to preach. After he finished preaching, there was an altar call for prayer, and I went up there with several other people. Then I began praying so hard because there were several things going on in my life that I needed God to intervene in. I was praying so hard the pastor told me to sit down because I was getting so weak, so I sat down. The service was dismissed, and people began leaving when the pastor asked me and my wife to meet him in his office so he could talk to us. In his office he began telling us things that were going on in my family that only God could have told him, things we never mentioned to anyone, and things we had no clue about. He was so pinpoint accurate about what was going on in our life that we stayed at that church for a year. After that year we began thinking about moving back to a church closer to where we lived. But our pastor was out of town on business, and he had an evangelist fill in for him until he returned. As the evangelist was preaching, he came to our bench where we were sitting and told us that my wife and I were thinking about leaving the church and how if we did we would be on our own, but if we stayed how God would bless us more than we could ever imagine and that God would tell us when it would be time to leave. So we stayed another year, and God sure did let me know when it was time to leave. Before we left that church, we were leaving to head back home from a Sunday morning service. When I got to Florida Boulevard in Baton Rouge, Louisiana, there was a hospital just to my right-hand side. God told me to go to that hospital because He had someone for me to pray for there. God sent me to the ICU on the third floor of that hospital. I walked around the halls for a little while. I asked God who He wanted me to pray for. I saw a lady sitting alone in the corner, and I went to talk to her. I asked her why she was there because God sent me to pray for someone. She told me how her daughter was in the ICU critically ill and on a breathing machine. The doctors told her how her daughter would more than likely never walk or talk again and be in a vegetative state for the rest of her life. I waited about ten minutes for the nurse to clear me to go in, and then we went in. I placed my hand on her forehead and prayed fervently. I said, "God, You created her in Your image. She is fearfully and wonderfully made. Your greatest wish is that she prosper and be in health even as our soul prospers. God, You said if we ask anything according to Your will, You hear us. And if we know You hear us, we have the petitions we ask for already granted. God, I'm asking a total healing for this lady. I'm asking that You heal her body from her head to her feet. Give her the strength to walk again and let her voice return again to her, because all Your ways are perfect and You are the greatest Healer Who ever was and ever will be. So I ask that You heal her completely." I headed home with my family after that. Six months later I saw the lady and her daughter walk into the church my family and I attended, and she stood up and testified about how God healed her daughter completely. It was another miracle to build faith in all who will believe.

The four girls each moved out when they became of age. Then we adopted our one-and-a-half-year-old granddaughter, McKinsey. When McKinsey was eight years old, we got stranded in heavy work traffic. When our 1989 Mercury Topaz with over two hundred thousand miles overheated on I-10 in Baton Rouge, Louisiana, I lifted the hood and prayed for God to provide water for the radiator. Just seconds later a pickup truck stopped beside us, and the driver handed me a five-gallon container of water and told me to keep it. I thanked him, and he drove off. When the engine cooled, we drove over two hundred miles to Jonesboro, Louisiana, to visit a friend for a few days. Our car did well. But on the way back at the halfway point, it began to sound like it was falling apart. I prayed, and the noise stopped. When we were ten miles away from our house, it began rattling again. So I got off the road, and everything went dead—no horn, no lights, no ignition. Nothing worked. Then we both prayed as the sun began to set. I told God, "You are the best Mechanic in the whole universe, and You can fix anything. Please help me get my family home before dark." We heard noises under the car after we prayed, as if things were coming back together. We waited a few minutes, and then the noises stopped. When I turned the key again, it started like it had a new battery and starter motor. We drove on home. Everything was perfect, and it stayed that way for months. An insurance agent told me before I got another vehicle that the Topaz had a –$600 value, but the insurance company gave me $800 after I was in a minor accident.

In my fifties I worked for an apartment complex, and part of my job was cleaning mold off air conditioner units. I became very ill for six months. I went from doctor to doctor, and I was only getting worse. I had low energy and pain throughout my body and would get very little sleep each night. I had carpal tunnel, rotator cuff pain, and hands and knees full of arthritis. I coughed a hundred times or more a day and had headaches and more. I turned it over to God and locked myself in my church at 10:00 p.m. for weeks and asked God for wisdom and understanding that my body would heal itself so I could help others. He showed me what to do, and my body was back to normal within thirty days. The prayer I prayed went like this:

"God, You created me in Your image. Genesis 1:27 says, 'So God created man in His own image, in the image of God created He him; male and female created He them.' You also said I am fearfully and wonderfully made in Psalm 139:14: 'I will praise thee; for I am fearfully and wonderfully made: marvelous are thy works; and that my soul knoweth right well.' You also said, Lord, that Your greatest wish is that I prosper and be in health in 3 John 2: 'Beloved, I wish above all things that thou mayest prosper and be in health, even as thy soul prospers.' You also said that if any man lack wisdom and ask, You will give it to them liberally in James 1:5: 'If any of you lack wisdom, let him ask of God, that giveth to all men liberally, and upbraideth not; and it shall be given him.' You also said if I ask anything according to Your will, You hear me. 1 John 5:14–15 says, 'And this is the confidence that we have in Him, that, if we ask anything according to His will He heareth us; and if we know that He hears us, whatsoever we ask, we know that we have the petitions that we desired of Him.' Also Your Word says in 1 John 3:22, 'And whatsoever we ask, we receive of Him, because we keep His commandments, and do those things that are pleasing in His sight.' So in the name of Jesus if Your Word says all this, then what I'm asking You right now is that You give me the wisdom and understanding so that my body will heal itself through Your Word. Help me to help myself so I can help others."

After I prayed this prayer, within thirty days my body was completely healed. One year later I saw one of the doctors whom I was seeing for my many illnesses. He was talking to another man, and I overheard his conversation. He mentioned me to the other gentleman, and he said, "I don't know where he went, what he did, or who he talked to. But that man had some serious medical problems. But I don't see a single thing wrong with him now." All the glory belongs to God! That's what I say because little is much when God is in it!

My wife and I were living in a mobile home in Gonzales, Louisiana, and an extremely violent storm passed through in the middle of the night. The winds were strong, and the rain was pouring. We were both sleeping when a large branch hanging high up overhead slammed into our roof right over our bed where we were sleeping and shook our whole trailer. Water started pouring down our walls underneath the bedroom window. Fortunately for us, it fell flat onto our roof and did not harm us, even though we were shaken up. When the rain had stopped the next morning, I went to inspect the roof and pushed the branch down to the ground. It was extremely waterlogged and heavy. I am so thankful to God for sparing us that night!

In October of 2014, I ordered a health supplement called coral calcium from a health food store in California for myself and a coworker. Both bottles were sealed but had been tampered with because both bottles were missing three or more capsules. We both became very ill. She took only one capsule and recovered slowly. I, however, took two of the pills a week later as recommended and became extremely ill. But thankfully I survived only by the grace of God. At Lafayette General Hospital in Lafayette, Louisiana, my blood pressure shot up to 334 over 132. Two nurses both told me that it was impossible to live with a blood pressure that high. 3 John 2 says, "Beloved, I wish above all things that thou mayest prosper and be in health, even as thy soul prospereth." Proverbs 4:20–22 says, "My son, attend to my words; incline thine ear unto my sayings. Let them not depart from thine eyes; keep them in the midst of thine heart. For they are life unto those that find them, and health to all their flesh." These scriptures tell me why it *is* possible when you're on a journey to Jesus.

I'll share with you the words of a song God gave me years ago during the darkest trial I've ever been through. The title of it is "Through the Eyes of Jesus":

> When I see the world, through the eyes of Jesus, I'll try to help someone today. I'll talk with kind words, say good things that I've heard. I'll even find more time to pray. When I see the world through the eyes of Jesus, no sin will reside

in my heart. The dark moves out when His light shines from within. It starts with only a spark. Though dark clouds will form, in the height of a storm, He's standing there with me. I feel no alarm. When I see the world through the eyes of Jesus, I'm taught how to walk on the sea. Though storms are raging, I put all my faith in the One Who's walking with me. When I see the world through the eyes of Jesus, I know He's walking with me. I know He's walking with me.

After God blessed me with several of these songs, one day I was at home with my wife and family, and we had a little poodle named Chico. Chico had become extremely ill and refused to eat or drink for days. We had to go to extreme measures to keep him from dehydrating. We were desperate for a healing in Chico's little body. So my wife told me to pray for him. That's exactly what I did. I put my hand on his little head and told God that He was the greatest Healer in the universe Who ever was and ever would be. I told God He could do anything. If He could heal humans, He could heal my dog, Chico. I believed that if it was His will for Chico to get better, then it was done. When I finished that prayer, I heard his breathing get very shallow, and he went into a deep sleep. I woke up around six thirty the next morning, and he wasn't moving. I began petting little Chico, and my wife stood by my side. Little Chico opened his eyes and jumped to his feet. He started barking and would not stop and ran from end to end of my eighty-foot-long trailer at full speed without stop. After running about twenty to twenty-five times from one end to the other, he lay down at our feet exhausted. We gave him fresh food and water, and he drank it all up. We all thanked God for this miracle.

In the mid-1980s I was still living with my mom, and we had a visitor one day. We got to a point in the conversation where he used a couple inappropriate words at the kitchen table. I made a comment saying that I didn't understand why some people blame God for everything that goes wrong in their life and never give Him credit for the things that do go right. The next morning my mom mentioned to me about how the statement I made brought tears to our visitor's eyes. I thought about that conversation several years later, and it inspired to write the following song called "Give God Credit." These are the words:

> Two brothers were brought up in fear. Life was a burden for their parents didn't care. Yet they grew up together. The older learned to pray. Now he became a preacher man, then began to say: Do you give God credit for things that go right? Or blame Him for all that's wrong in your life? Stained on the cross was royal blood He shed. Do you give God credit? That's what he said. His brother was drifting in sin, crime, and the jury gave him time inside the pen. He came so close to freedom but chose a bloody knife. The preacher, still his closest friend, could only give advice: Do you give God credit for things that go right? Or blame Him for all that's wrong in your life? Stained on the cross was royal blood He shed. Do you give God credit? That's what he said. His brother now cursed every door. There at the prison threw a Bible to the floor. Suddenly a sound came, the tolling of a bell. Some say he gave his life to God. Time will only tell. Did he give God credit for things that go right or blame Him for all that's wrong in his life? God proved His love. Royal blood He shed. Did he give God credit? big brother said. Did he give God credit? That's what he said.

When I was still working at that chemical plant, one day I had just returned from the post office with the company mail. I got back to the plant and parked the van and was heading to go back inside. I walked right beside the flagpole, and I was only about two or so feet from it. The weather was bad out with terrible lightning and thunder. I only had a few more steps to go to get inside. Three or four seconds later after I passed by the flagpole, lightning struck it, and the thunder roared. I could have been struck by lightning and killed, but God had other plans. He spared me once again!

While we were still going to the church in Gonzales, Louisiana, my wife and I heard some bad news. A member of the church whom we knew well was in a very serious automobile accident. The doctors said it would take a miracle for him to survive; he was in such critical condition. After the church sent up much prayer to heaven for his recovery, the doctors began to see some progress in him as time went on. Finally, after many weeks in the hospital, he finally had the opportunity to go home. But he was paralyzed from the waist down. He had to stay in a wheelchair. He had four children and a wife, but bad news came his way. After a year or so, his wife left him for another man because of his paralysis, and it devastated him. When I visited him after she left, he looked at me and said, "Allen, I want you to write me a song." I told him I would be happy to and asked if he had a title in mind he would like to use. He said yes and said, "You Got What You Wanted but Lost What You Had." That's the title of this next song I will tell you. Here are the words:

> On the day of our vows, I knew you to be the perfect wife. You'd be the mother of my child, who'd melt my heart with only just a smile. Suddenly a tragedy hurt the family bad. You packed your bags to go away. Well, you got what you wanted but lost what you had. Like a rose in its bloom, you soon had attention come your way. You found it in another man who handed you a fancy word bouquet. An offer for a better life, a chance at any fad. A clever plan to win your hand. Well, you got what you wanted but lost what you had. So I'll raise the kids, give them care. Tie their shoes, comb their hair. Just

remember them in prayer. God gave them to you too. I'll cling to what I have. The Lord is my Shepherd day or night. Every trial that I've been through is like a tunnel. At the end there's light. I'm holding to a rainbow I know will never fade. I wish that you had held on too. Well, you got what you wanted but lost what you had. So I'll raise the kids, give them care. Tie their shoes, comb their hair. Just remember them in prayer. God gave them to you too. I'll cling to what I have. The Lord is my Shepherd day or night. Every trial that I've been through is like a tunnel. At the end there's light. I'm holding onto a rainbow I know will never fade. I wish that you had held on too. Well, you got what you wanted but lost what you had. Yes, you got what you wanted but lost what you had.

This next testimony is how God used me to help a homeless stranger hitchhiking across North America. I was on my way back home from New Orleans, Louisiana. And when I got about a mile or two from my exit, I saw this man who was about twenty years old on I-10. I slowed down and passed him up. I got about a hundred yards ahead of him, and I tried picking up speed, but God told me to go back and pick him up. So I pulled over and waited for him. I saw him running toward my vehicle. He got in and thanked me for stopping and told me he was very hungry. We took the next exit, which led to where I lived, which was about eight miles down the road. I took him to a local restaurant and told him to order anything he wanted regardless of the price. He thanked me for the meal, and I offered him more, but he ate all he could. He asked if there was any way he could pay me back. I told him I had nothing personal he could help me with, but he could help me set up for the church service I was attending the next day. He could help me sweep the floors, place the chairs where they went, and clean the parking lot outside. I gave him the $35 I had in my wallet and gave him a small Bible that I had.

He was very appreciative of everything I had done, and he asked if I could take him back to the interstate where I had picked him up from, and I was happy to. He thanked me again and said he would never forget me. I prayed over him for his safety, and I let him out close to the exit. I never saw him again after that. After I helped that man, I only had a quarter of a tank of gas left. I had enough gas to get home that evening, but that was it. Over the next three weeks, I kept looking at my gas gauge, and it always stayed at a quarter of a tank. I drove around a lot those three weeks, and not once did I ever run out of gas. When I finally asked why it was never going down, that's when it started going down. If I had only kept the faith, there's no telling how far God would've carried me on just a quarter of a tank of gas.

I was working at a chemical plant years later, and one day I had barely any gas in my tank—it was almost on empty. One of the pipe fitters I knew came to the warehouse to pick up the tools I had to issue to them, and we started talking about my old car. He asked me if I made it home with very little gas, and I told him yes. I informed him that I was gonna go back home again with very little gas. It was below empty. I had to drive all the way home. I said to myself if it got me home on empty, it could do it again. So I went back to the plant the next day, and the pipe fitter asked if I made it back on empty. I did. Then I started it and drove all the way to Gonzales, Louisiana, again with still a few miles to drive. The car ran out of fuel right in front of a place that I worked at a few years earlier. The office door was closed, but I saw someone in the back of the building. We walked toward each other, and he asked if I needed anything. I told him how I needed a little bit of gas as I had run out. He brought me a can of gas, and I put enough in my tank to get home, and I thanked him. When I got near a gas station near my home, I fueled back up and drove home. I thanked God for blessing me and getting me home safely.

After I got married, I was somewhere in my forties when I accepted a part-time job near Donaldsonville, Louisiana, cleaning a building at a power plant. I would go in at 9:30 p.m. and leave around 11:00 p.m. After I closed the doors and locked up to leave,

I was walking to my car and it was late at night when God spoke to me. He said, "Be extremely careful on your way back home. If you are not careful, you may not ever see your family again." I drove about ten miles and stopped at a four-way stop on an old country road. There was a truck ahead of me, and we met at the four-way stop. I got to the stop sign about twenty seconds before he did, but I was going to let him go ahead of me anyways. They didn't go, so I made my turn to the right. Where I lived was only a couple hundred yards ahead of me. There were two men in the truck. They got right on my bumper when I made my turn, no more than a foot or two behind me. I turned into the trailer park where my family and I lived at the time, and I went a short piece forward and stopped after about thirty feet. I approached the passenger side door thinking they needed directions. I asked them if they needed any help. One man pulled a firearm out of his shirt and cocked it back. He didn't say a word. The other man got out of the truck and went around the back and just stood there. He looked at me and pointed his firearm and then fired a shot at the road. He then pointed his firearm again right at me and said, "Nobody cuts in front of us and gets away with it!" He again pointed his weapon right at me, and I prayed in my mind, asking God to place angels around me and protect me. I thought he was going to shoot me in the back when I turned, but he put his weapon down. I apologized to him, and as I was walking back to my trailer, they pulled out very slowly and kept on watching me very closely. The next morning I was getting ready for work, and that same truck with three people this time pulled up behind my mobile home. They saw me and my daughters looking through the blinds, just trying to get their license plate number. They saw us, and they peeled out extremely fast, throwing rocks and dust everywhere as they sped off. I notified the police, and they tried to find that truck. I saw them again about a week later while on the road, but they never recognized me because I was in a different vehicle and had my sun visor all the way down. That was the last I have ever seen of them. Once again, God showed me that He's always there for me! After this experience God blessed me with a song that has helped many people and myself over the years. The title of this song is "Sin Has No Hope." These are the words:

> We all know of someone we never could trust. In our world there are dangers so common to us. Every door shut by fear and all terror and crime are reminders that sin is the sign of our times. Sin has no hope when God is our way. There's a brighter tomorrow, a better today. The wolf shall dwell with the lamb. Hate will change into smiles. Sin has no hope, with the Lord and His child. If sin was abandoned, no prison we'd need. There would be no rebellion, no liars or thieves. Weapons would never prosper. All fighting would end. Love would bloom like a flower. All heartaches would mend. Sin has no hope when God is our way. There's a brighter tomorrow, a better today. The wolf shall dwell with the lamb. Hate will change into smiles. Sin has no hope, with the Lord and His child. If sin was abandoned, no prison we'd need. There would be no rebellion, no liars or thieves. Weapons would never prosper. All fighting would end. Love would bloom like a flower. All heartaches would mend. Sin has no hope when God is our way. There's a brighter tomorrow, a better today. The wolf shall dwell with the lamb. Hate will change into smiles. Sin has no hope, with the Lord and His child. Sin has no hope, with the Lord and His child.

In the mid-1990s, God blessed me with another song. It has been a joy to sing this song in the various places I've been. This song has helped me throughout my journey to Jesus. The title of this song is "I Gotta Look More to Jesus." These are the words:

> The road of life is a winding road, but Jesus is my guide. Through valleys and the dark hills,

He walks along my side. And if I touch a thorn or two, He's there if I should fall. I gotta look more to Jesus to see me through it all. He's my rainbow, and where I go He's closer than a friend. I gotta look more to Jesus before my journey ends. Sometimes I feel like a broken wheel on the road I'm headed down. I'm cornered in a stormy wind. My faith is on the ground. But Jesus picks me up again. I'm nothing on my own. I gotta look more to Jesus to lead me safely home. He's my rainbow, and where I go He's closer than a friend. I gotta look more to Jesus before my journey ends. I gotta look more to Jesus before my journey ends.

I was driving back to my hometown of Lutcher, Louisiana, for one of my singings I had scheduled. But I was stopped because of a Christmas parade in progress. I watched the entire parade, and what I noticed was despite all the beautiful decorations, not once did I see a single nativity scene depicting the birth of Jesus. I asked myself, "Where's the Christ child?" With that thought, I knew I instantly had another song in the works. These are the words:

Parades are now starting. Bands are all marching. People are parking everywhere. Santa is waving. Children are craving candy he's throwing through the air. But where is the Christ child? Where is the King? What is the real joy Christmas brings? What is the reason that the angels sing? What is the reason that the angels sing? There's fire trucks and limousines, green trees with candy canes. Reindeer are ready with their sleigh. Horses with little elves, floats lined with silver bells. Fun for the family through the day. But where is the Christ child? Where is the King? What is the real joy Christmas brings? What is the reason that the angels sing? What is the reason that the angels sing? Now every December the floats show their splendor. Glitter with colors of the fall. Signs of the season, but they're not the reason to wish Merry Christmas to all. So where is the Christ child? Where is the King? What is the real joy Christmas brings? What is the reason that the angels sing? What is the reason that the angels sing? So where is the Christ child? Where is the King? What is the real joy Christmas brings? What is the reason that the angels sing? What is the reason that the angels sing?

A few years back, God gave me another Christmas song. My family and I were attending a church in Crowley, Louisiana, where we lived at the time. And the pastor gave his closing words before he dismissed us, and his words caught my attention. After he finished speaking, I just knew God had given me a title for a new Christmas song He wanted me to write. The title of that song is "Hold On to the Hand That Is Hope." These are the words:

With Christmas appearing, more music I'm hearing, the drama team sharing their joy for the Lord. More singing and laughter. A word from the pastor, assuring us all, reminding what everything's for. Hold on to the hand that is hope, hope forever. Never let go of mercy and grace. Hold on to the hand that is hope, hope forever. Hold on to the hand that is hope, whatever you face. A new year approaching, more people are boasting, somewhere they are toasting, whiskey or wine. But I'm more excited that I've been invited to feast with our King. I'm holding a promise divine! Hold on to the hand that is hope, hope forever. Never let go of mercy and grace. Hold on to the hand that is hope, hope forever. Hold on to the hand that is hope, whatever you face. Are you hurting? Need a friend? He waits at your door. Let Him in! He'll restore and heal, to build your faith! Hold on to the hand that is hope, whatever you face! Hold on to the hand that is hope, whatever you face!

Sometimes, God has to shake me up to wake me up. I even thank God for all the times He's corrected me when I was wrong. I woke up one morning to get ready for work and drive to the chemical plant that I worked at, at that time, which was about fifteen miles away. I got in my car to go to work, and my car wouldn't shift when I got out of the parking lot to the main road. I had to pull over into a convenience store parking lot to check the transmission fluid. It took about three or four minutes to check it. When I checked it, everything was at the levels they needed to be, so I got back in my car and drove off to head back to work. Part of my drive to work I had to drive a long dark stretch about four or five miles long. My headlights needed to be changed because they were very dim. There was an eighteen-wheeler that broke down in the distance. It had no working headlights or taillights or reflectors in place. Right before I got to it, someone was coming around the truck with some reflectors in hand to place on the road. I slowed down quickly. Then I realized that God allowed my shift to not work properly for a reason. Once again, He spared me from what could have been another tragedy. I thank God for keeping His hand upon me that day. There's never a day that goes by that He hasn't shown His unending love to me.

Another great song God has blessed me with is one that I have been blessed to sing at a couple churches before. When I sang it at the church in Baton Rouge, Louisiana, that my family and I attended at the time, the spirit of God fell so strongly in that place that there wasn't any preaching, just an hour-long prayer meeting. The title of this next song is "There's a Name." These are the words:

There's a name greater than every other name, greater than other names can be. Every tongue will confess the name of Jesus. Since I love that name, it's no problem for me. There's a name that can wash every sin away, free the soul that's been bound and chained. There's a name that all power's been given to. It is Jesus Who will forever reign. No other name is given, under heaven, written in the Word of God, whereby we must be saved. That is why I want to praise His name. There's a name, one I've learned to depend upon, through the storms or when everything's right. There's a name that will stand throughout all the ages, like the pages in the Lamb's Book of Life! There's a name that will stand throughout all the ages, like the pages in the Lamb's Book of Life! There's a name that can wash every sin away, free the soul that's been bound and chained. There's a name that all power's been given to. It is Jesus Who will forever reign. No other name is given, under heaven, written in the Word of God, whereby we must be saved. That is why I want to praise His name. There's a name, one I've learned to depend upon, through the storms or when everything's right. There's a name that will stand throughout all the ages, like the pages in the Lamb's Book of Life! There's a name that will stand throughout all the ages, like the pages in the Lamb's Book of Life! Like the pages in the Lamb's Book of Life!

One thing I've learned in my life and relationship with God is regardless of the things I've done and no matter the situation I may be in, if I ever need help from God, all I have to do is call upon the name of Jesus and He's there. I have several Bible verses that I love to quote that prove Who He is. They are the following:

Philippians 2:9 states, "His name is above every name." Proverbs 18:10 says, "His name is a strong tower." Acts 2:38 explains the plan of salvation for us. It says, "Then Peter said unto them, repent and be baptized every one of you in the name of Jesus Christ for the remission of sins and you shall receive the gift of the Holy Ghost." Then Acts 4:12 explains that Jesus's name is the *only* name that can save. It says, "Neither is there salvation in any other: For there is none other name under Heaven given among men whereby we must be saved." Colossians 2:9–10 talks about who we are through *Him*. It says, "For in Him dwelleth all the fullness of the Godhead bodily. And ye are complete in Him, which is the head of all principality and power." All these scriptures tell me what His name is and exactly Who He is. If the Bible is the infallible Word of God and God is truth, I trust Him to be Who He says He is and who He says I am. I am who I am because the I Am tells me who I am! The title of the next song is 'Strength, Song, and Salvation.' Psalm 118:14 states, 'The Lord is my strength and song, and has become my salvation.'

> The Lord is my strength. The Lord is my song. He's become my salvation. To Him I belong. The Rock of all ages, my Shield from the storms. The Lord is my strength. The Lord is my song. His Word's like a sword, piercing my bones, to guide and protect me, till heaven's my home. Reaching the lost, the heart of His plan. Build on the rock, not on the sand. The Lord is my strength. The Lord is my song. He's become my salvation. To Him I belong. The Rock of all ages, my Shield from the storms. The Lord is my strength. The Lord is my song. His Word's like a sword, piercing my bones, to guide and protect me, till heaven's my home. Reaching the lost, the heart of His plan. Build on the rock, not on the sand. The Lord is my strength. The Lord is my song.

Without a doubt, the most anointed song God has ever blessed me with is called "Mission on the Hill." I prayed about this song as God led me through it. I worked on this song for several weeks before I felt it was the way God wanted it. These are the words:

> Do you falsely accuse Him? Now will you abuse the man with a plan to fulfill? Take a look as they mock Him. They cannot stop Him. His mission on Calvary's hill. Feel all the agony; just hear the sound. He's nailed to the cross. It's fixed in the ground. Did you kneel at His feet as His blood was shed? Or help place the thorns on His head? From the cross to the cave where the Savior was laid. Soon He'd arise from that grave. In triumph and victory, His mission at Calvary! But look at the price that He paid! Feel all the agony; just hear the sound. He's nailed to the cross. It's fixed in the ground. Did you kneel at His feet as His blood was shed? Or help place the thorns on His head? He's the same God today with a plan to fulfill! His child to abide in His will. Tell the world He is risen! Do you need a vision? Look back at Calvary's hill! Feel all the agony; just hear the sound. He's nailed to the cross. It's fixed in the ground. Did you kneel at His feet as His blood was shed? Or help place the thorns on His head? Our Savior is risen. Do you need a vision? Look back at Calvary's hill! He's the same God today with a plan we should stay with! Reaching the world is His will! Our Savior is risen. Do you need a vision? Look back at Calvary's hill! Our Savior is risen. Do you need a vision? Look back at Calvary's hill!

This next song God blessed me with in 2020. I love this song because it explains why we are important to Jesus. The title of it is "Important to Jesus." These are the words:

> We know He's the Potter, we are the clay. God values His children. Many will stray. Our praise He inhabits. Our tears He retains. Important to Jesus, every face, every name. Important to Jesus, the apple of His eye. More precious than gold, the soul of His child. Obeying God's Word, the heavenly prize! The gateway to glory, to be with His bride. Important to Jesus, to be with His bride. The faithful and ready go through their trials. They walk in the Spirit; God shows them how. He walks on the water, spares from the deep! Important to Jesus, His promise He'll keep. Important to Jesus, the apple of His eye. More precious than gold, the soul of His child. Obeying God's Word, the heavenly prize! The gateway to glory, to be with His bride. Important to Jesus, to be with His bride. Rubies have value. Pearls bring their price. Our King charged us nothing, to lay down His life. From there up to glory, where angels reside. He'll soon be returning to call home His bride. Important to Jesus, the apple of His eye. More precious than gold, the soul of His child. Obeying God's Word, the heavenly prize! The gateway to glory, to be with His bride. Important to Jesus, to be with His bride.

This next song is a song God gave me years ago. The title of it is "He's the Reason." It explains how God is literally the reason for our existence and why everything is the way it is. It talks about His beautiful creation and the great sacrifice He made on the cross at Calvary. These are the words:

> Why do the flowers bloom, in spring and in the summertime? Trees are full of color in the fall. Then winter brings the sleet and snow. Cold, cold winds blow. There's a reason. God's the reason for it all. The reason why stars are in the heavens, why fishes in the deep. His Word I want to keep. For He shed His blood for me, on the cross at Calvary. He's the reason. He's the reason why I'm free. I see a rainbow in the sky along the highway. A billboard sign I'm reading: pray for peace. I see as I go down a bridge the church high on a ridge. There's a reason. God's the reason for it all. The reason why stars are in the heavens, why fishes in the deep. His Word I want to keep. For He shed His blood for me, on the cross at Calvary. He's the reason. He's the reason why I'm free. As I arrive and go, inside the church I'm hearing prayer. There's healing and revival in the air. I hear rejoicing in a room, sinners coming home. There's a reason. God's the reason for it all. The reason why stars are in the heavens, why fishes in the deep. His Word I want to keep. For He shed His blood for me, on the cross at Calvary. He's the reason. He's the reason why I'm free. Yes, He shed His blood for me, on the cross at Calvary. He's the reason. He's the reason why I'm free.

God gave me this song while I was still living in the Gonzales, Louisiana, area. I have always loved this song as has everyone else who has heard the song. Just like every other Christian song I have written, God has always guided me through the process of the entire song. The name of this song is "The Choice Is Mine." These are the words:

> I'll never choose a better book. The Bible's where I need to look. For my salvation, it's there for me. I can turn to the cross at Calvary. The choice is mine to serve the Lord. He's the One worth living for. The choice is clear when I must choose. With God I'll never lose. The choice is clear when I must choose. With God I'll never lose. The devil will say do or don't. It's up to me to say I won't. He knows he's doomed and will never win. I can trust in the Lord and follow Him. The choice is mine to serve the Lord. He's the One worth living for. The choice is clear when I must choose. With God I'll never lose. The choice is clear when I must choose. With God I'll never lose. What will I buy? What will I wear? Decisions daily fill the air. There's one that will lead me to heaven's door. I am lost without God, you can be sure! The choice is mine to serve the Lord. He's the One worth living for. The choice is clear when I must choose. With God I'll never lose. The choice is clear when I must choose. With God I'll never lose.

God blessed me with this next song that I have sung many times over the years. It has blessed so many people, myself included. The title of this song is "It's in the Book." These are the words:

> I've always liked great stories, so I knew just where to look. The Bible has the stories. I found them in the Book. Great miracles by Jesus led sinners to be saved. There's pages on the prophets and the courage they displayed. It's in the Book. It's in the Book. In the written Word of God, the

greatest stories ever told are in the Book. They're in the Book. I read of Saul's conversion; he was blinded by the light. And Gideon's great army, their victory in the night.

Commandments God gave Moses on tablets made of stone. And Daniel in the lion's den and the faith that he had shown. It's in the Book. It's in the Book. In the written Word of God, the greatest stories ever told are in the Book. They're in the Book.

A chapter about Isaac and father Abraham. There's verses on the Christ child, His birth at Bethlehem. The story of deliverance as God opened up the sea. The story of redemption on the cross at Calvary. It's in the Book. It's in the Book. In the written Word of God, the greatest stories ever told are in the Book. They're in the Book. The story of deliverance as God opened up the sea. The story of redemption on the cross at Calvary. It's in the Book. They're in the Book. A chapter about Isaac and father Abraham. There's verses on the Christ child, His birth at Bethlehem. The story of deliverance as God opened up the sea. The story of redemption on the cross at Calvary. It's in the Book. It's in the Book. In the written Word of God, the greatest stories ever told are in the Book. They're in the Book. A chapter about Isaac and father Abraham. There's verses on the Christ child, His birth at Bethlehem. The story of deliverance as God opened up the sea. The story of redemption on the cross at Calvary. It's in the Book. It's in the Book. In the written Word of God, the greatest stories ever told are in the Book. They're in the Book. It's in the Book. They're in the Book.

This next song God gave me is one of my more different Christian-style songs. A lot of other people who have heard this song really like it. This song tells us exactly Who He is and what He can and will do for us if we believe! The title of this song is "Does God Need an Education?" These are the words:

> Does God need an education? A tutor guide His hand? Oh, who is it can counsel Him or make Him understand? For if He can heal my flesh and bone and His finger carve in stone. Oh, what He can do for me and you. He's God and God alone! Does God need an education, in science or chemistry? To form a man from dust and then provide his every need. God provided food like fowl above and the fishes in the deep. He gave man a wife and the bread of life. God's Word for man to keep. He numbers the hairs that are on our head. Every star in the heavens He names. He's the same today as yesterday. Forever and ever He reigns. Does God need an education to learn what's best for me? What school? What course? God is the source, of life eternally. For His PhD is love and grace. For He pardons all our sins. They are washed away when we obey His Word and live for Him. His PhD is love and grace. For He pardons all our sins. They are washed away when we obey His Word and live for Him.

One of my more recent testimonies involves my adult daughter McKinsey who still lives at home with us. She and I were sitting at the kitchen table just talking. She had been having dizzy spells all day and was feeling unwell. I looked away for just a moment and heard a loud crashing sound. I looked and saw my daughter passed out on the floor. I hollered for my wife to call 911, and I ran to her side. She stopped breathing, and I immediately began fervently praying over her. And not even a minute after that, she regained consciousness. I took her to the hospital, and they took her vitals. We found out that her blood pressure bottomed out at 87/52, but her pulse was dangerously high for her at 102. Today she is healthy and thriving! I thank God for reviving her and keeping His hand over her! All the glory belongs to Him and Him alone!

God gave me this next song in the mid-1990s. It talks about how in the good times and in the bad God sees everything we go through on a daily basis. The title of this song is "It's All before His Eyes." These are the words:

> God sees every baby born. He knows when someone dies. He's there where good and evil are. It's all before His eyes. All our ways, all our days, and everything we do, He's watching me and you. It's all before His eyes. We're all before His eyes. Who can run or hide from Him? Why we even try? The hairs are numbered on our heads. It's all before His eyes. All our ways, all our days, and everything we do, He's watching me and you. It's all before His eyes. We're all before His eyes. Things we do to hurt someone, we surely won't get by. For what we give and how we live, it's all before His eyes. All our ways, all our days, and everything we do, He's watching me and you. It's all before His eyes. We're all before His eyes. It's all before His eyes.

This next song God blessed me with back in the mid-1990s. It talks about our very reason for existence. The title of it is "I Tell Them." These are the words:

> I had gone to an old time revival. In a tent on the floor I heard the Word. It seemed like my soul had entered heaven. God told me to tell others what I heard. So I tell them the Good Word of Jesus. I tell them He'll soon be returning again. In a moment in the twinkling of an eye He'll

appear. I tell them all who will hear. I tell them all who will hear. Now I read from the pages of my Bible and learn from the Good Word of the Lord. His will is to tell the Word to others. Yes, heaven could be their great reward. I tell them the Good Word of Jesus. I tell them He'll soon be returning again. In a moment in the twinkling of an eye He'll appear. I tell them all who will hear.

I tell them the Good Word of Jesus. I tell them He'll soon be returning again. In a moment in the twinkling of an eye He'll appear. I tell them all who will hear. I tell them all who will hear.

One of my more earlier songs God has blessed me with is called "Hope Will Take You Home." It has been a blessing to many people over the years. Everywhere I have sung this song, I have gotten quite a reaction from it. These are the words:

When life gets in a circle and nothing seems to work well, hold on; hope will take you home. Take you through your problems, give you faith to solve them. Hold on; hope will take you home. Hope will take you home to Jesus. He'll occupy a room inside your heart. Hope will take you home to Jesus. Loving Him is where we need to start. When you expect a miracle, do you find the climb uphill? Hold on; hope will take you home. The key is in believing, not in doubt or grieving. Hold on; hope will take you home. Hope will take you home to Jesus. He'll occupy a room inside your heart. Hope will take you home to Jesus. Loving Him is where we need to start.

Life will have some valleys, dark roads, and alleys. Hold on; hope will take you home. Down the road you're charting, the end will be rewarding. Hold on; hope will take you home. Hope will take you home to Jesus. He'll occupy a room inside your heart. Hope will take you home to Jesus. Loving Him is where we need to start. Hope will take you home to Jesus. He'll occupy a room inside your heart. Hope will take you home to Jesus. Loving Him is where we need to start. Loving Him is where we need to start.

I believe it was back in the 1980s when I was working at a heavy equipment plant. I was bringing some parts to the service department, and there were about five men eating their lunch near some heavy machinery they were servicing. I brought them the parts they needed, and I was chewed out lower than a dog. In the softest and kindest tone I could use, I apologized for being late with their order and promised to be on time in the future. Everyone went quiet, and I walked away. The following morning the same man saw me in the hallway and began pushing past everyone else to get to me to tell me good morning. The Bible states in Proverbs 15:1, "A soft answer turneth away wrath: but grievous words stir up anger."

This next song God blessed me with a few years back. It talks about how even though we go through tragedies and trials, God can and always will bring us through them and use them for our good! The title of this song is "For His Purpose." Part of the inspiration for putting this song in my book stems from one of my favorite scriptures in the Bible. It can be found in Romans 8:28, "And we know that all things work together for good to them that love God, to them who are the called according to his purpose." These are the words:

> For His purpose God put fire on the mountain, storms upon the surface of the sea. God called Peter out onto the water, spared him from the dangers of the deep. For His purpose God will turn away a tragedy. A shepherd boy with sling and stones had victory. If God can cause the lame to walk, even make a donkey talk, what do you think He'd do for you and me? What do you

think He'd do for you and me? For His purpose God had ravens feed Elijah. A shout at Jericho brought down the wall. Daniel in the den of lions was fearless. An angel there beside him through it all. For His purpose God will turn away a tragedy. A shepherd boy with sling and stones had victory. If God can cause the lame to walk, even make a donkey talk, what do you think He'd do for you and me? What do you think He'd do for you and me? For God's purpose Noah built an ark of safety, saved himself and all his family. Now God has an ark of grace and mercy, because of blood He shed at Calvary. For His purpose God will turn away a tragedy. A shepherd boy with sling and stones had victory. If God can cause the lame to walk, even make a donkey talk, what do you think He'd do for you and me? What do you think He'd do for you and me? For God's purpose, what He'd do for you and me!

There are many verses in the Bible talking about God's healing power. I wanted to write a song about it, so I prayed, and God gave me one. The title of it is "The Healer's in the House." These are the words:

An old time revival sawdust on the floor. Flowers near the pulpit, people to the door. Benches are the altar for sinners praying through, and banners read overheard, "The Healer's Here for You." The Healer's in the house. In the congregation, praise Him with a shout! He's moving about! Pouring out salvation! The Healer's in the house! The Healer's in the house! A man walking toward me handing out a card. Speaking loud and clearly, "Do you know the Lord? God will make that mountain a pebble at your feet."

Let's both agree and say amen! He then begins to preach! The Healer's in the house. In the congregation, praise Him with a shout! He's moving about! Pouring out salvation! The Healer's in the house! The Healer's in the house! I kneel at the altar thinking it's a dream! Visions of an angel with a tambourine, standing right beside me waiting to rejoice! As I repent of all my sins, again I hear a voice! The Healer's in the house. In the congregation, praise Him with a shout! He's moving about! Pouring out salvation! The Healer's in the house! The Healer's in the house!

A lady came up to me while I was at work around 2015 when my family and I still lived in Crowley, Louisiana. She asked me how I got my prayers answered, and I told her we need to make sure we're living a life that's pleasing to God. In the New Testament in the Bible, 2 Peter 3:9 states, "The Lord is not slack concerning his promise, as some men count slackness; but is longsuffering to us-ward, not willing that any should perish, but that all should come to repentance." Then in 1 John 3:22, the Bible says, "And whatsoever we ask, we receive of him, because we keep his commandments, and do those things that are pleasing in his sight." Jesus said in the New Testament that we are to believe in Him through their (His disciples) words and what He taught them for three-and-a-half years. 1 John 4:6 says, "We are of God: he that knoweth God heareth us; he that is not of God heareth not us. Hereby know we the spirit of truth, and the spirit of error."

Back when I was still living in Gonzales, Louisiana, God gave me a song in a dream. I woke up at 6:30 a.m. to quickly write down the words. The title of the song is "Someday." These are the words:

There's a better day ahead, a better world we'll see. People everywhere are friends. There's peace and harmony. Someday, someday very soon, no pain, no tears. No trouble or fears. For the children of the King, when Jesus comes again, someday very soon, someday very soon. Not a thief will be around. No need to lock your doors. Honesty and love abound. A better day's in store.

Someday, someday very soon, no pain, no tears. No trouble or fears. For the children of the King, when Jesus comes again, someday very soon, someday very soon. No drugs upon our street, no sin throughout the land. Only those who love the Lord will fit into His plan. Someday, someday very soon, no pain, no tears. No trouble or fears. For the children of the King, when Jesus comes again, someday very soon, someday very soon.

There are a lot of people who believe that there isn't a God Who can heal, save, and deliver people from their circumstances. But not only do I think that there is but I *know* that there is a God Who can do all that and more! His name is Jesus, and He is alive and sitting on the throne! This next song talks about how regardless of all the chaos going on in our world, He is still alive!

They can take God off our money, say Jesus was a Jew, Who prophesied and then He died, a man they never knew. Denying all His power and saying He never did a thing. Well, that won't change the fact He's coming back again! Alive, He's alive! Like lightning in the sky, as rushing mighty wind, with Holy Ghost fire! He's the God of all creation. In His hands there's true salvation. He's alive! He's alive! Do you think He's dead and buried, behind that wall of stone? And left man in his misery, to die or be alone? Imagine no religion, no devil or a burning hell! Well, that won't change the fact Jesus is alive and well! Alive, He's alive! Like lightning in the sky, as rushing mighty wind, with Holy Ghost fire! He's the God of all creation. In His hands there's true salvation. He's alive! He's alive! They can padlock all the churches. The trumpet still will sound! God shall descend into the clouds, with angels all around! I'd rather give Him glory than turn away and live in sin! Hey, hold onto your hat! He's coming back again! Alive, He's alive! Like lightning in the sky, as rushing mighty wind, with Holy Ghost fire! He's the God of all creation. In His hands there's true salvation. He's alive! He's alive!

"When Jesus Speaks" is my most recent song God has blessed me with. Psalm 96:1 says, "O sing unto the Lord a new song: sing unto the Lord, all the earth." Then Colossians 3:16 states, "Let the word of Christ dwell in you richly in all wisdom; teaching and admonishing one another in psalms and hymns and spiritual songs, singing with grace in your hearts to the Lord."

When Jesus speaks, there's peace in the valley. Mountains will be pebbles at our feet. His voice thunders out of the heavens for all who will believe when Jesus speaks. When Jesus speaks, there's hope in a tragedy. Promise in the Word that He will keep. Faith brings the miracle of healing to all who will believe when Jesus speaks. Anything can happen when Jesus speaks. He'll cast demons into swine. There's healing for the blind. Water turns to wine, when Jesus speaks.

All things are possible. His power, unstoppable. His Word, reliable. When Jesus speaks. When Jesus speaks, there's hope for the sinner. Promise in the Word for all to read. God gave Peter keys of the kingdom. It's time to claim the promise and believe. Anything can happen when Jesus speaks. He'll cast demons into swine. There's healing for the blind. Water turns to wine, when Jesus speaks. All things are possible. His power, unstoppable. His Word, reliable. When Jesus speaks. It's time to claim your promise and believe when Jesus speaks. It's time to claim your promise and believe when Jesus speaks.

I thank Him for He has blessed me abundantly since then on my journey to Jesus. I give Him all the glory, praise, and honor for the songs and testimonies He has given me since that day in July of 1981 and then all throughout the years since then. It is a privilege and honor to be able to live a life that pleases Him!

Psalm 139:9–10 says, "If I take the wings of the morning, and dwell in the uttermost parts of the sea; Even there shall thy hand lead me, and thy right hand shall hold me." This next song God gave me sometime in the early 1990s. The title of it is "Never Out of Reach." These are the words:

> I could be a million miles from the nearest telephone. Far away from family, far away from home. God is closer than a brother watching over me. He's never out of reach when I'm in need. Even on the valley floor when I felt I had no friend. Seemed like I could only lose, never had a win. Victory was just ahead when I met God in prayer. He's never out of reach, not anywhere. If I could climb a rainbow He'd still be in my reach. Standing in my shadow, watching over me. He's my anchor in the deep. I'm a vessel in His hand. Sailing of the sea of life, for the promise land. Just in front of me, I see the harbor of His grace. He's never out of reach in any place. I'm never out of reach of God's love!

I remember years ago I was invited to sing at a flea market in Prairieville, Louisiana. There were at least a hundred booths and vendors there. At least two to three hundred people were shopping and walking around. I got set up and ready to begin singing as people were passing by. I got to about my seventh or eighth song when a group of five or six teenagers passed by and began heckling me, telling me to shut up and that no one wanted to hear any of my singing. Words alone couldn't describe how I felt from the sting of their words. I stumbled and struggled through my next and last song before deciding to pick it all up and call it quits for the evening. No sooner than I had started picking up all my equipment, the vendors in the area began to come tell me one by one how thankful and appreciative they were of me singing and how blessed they were by the songs God blessed me with. Then the owner of the flea market came by before I left and thanked me for coming and singing. He handed me $100. I told him I didn't ask for any money for my time. I just did it because God blessed me with a song ministry called "Songs for Jesus" that many people were thankful for and blessed by.

This next song God gave me in the mid- to late 1990s. I was then living in the Prairieville, Louisiana, area at the time. The title of it is "Fall on the Rock." These are the words:

> The seagulls are flying over the bay. Along on the pier he prays. There's a ship on the harbor. The moon's on the water. He closes his Bible and says, "Fall on the Rock, Jesus the Rock. Fall on the Rock of creation. Don't build on the sand. Fall while you can. Fall on the Rock of salvation." A young fiery preacher from South Illinois, he moved to the bay as a boy. Mom was a teacher, his dad a preacher. They taught him the ways of the Lord. Fall on the Rock, Jesus the Rock. Fall on the Rock of creation. Don't build on the sand. Fall while you can. Fall on the Rock of salvation. From the church on the ridge to White River Bridge, he preached along the shore. He stood like a martyr, his voice on the water. No demon dared enter his door. Fall on the Rock, Jesus the Rock. Fall on the Rock of creation. Don't build on the sand. Fall while you can. Fall on the Rock

of salvation. Don't build on the sand. Fall while you can. Fall on the Rock of salvation.

Back in the mid-1980s, I went to the post office one day, and I got a hate letter in the mail. I sat down at a desk back at home in Lutcher, Louisiana. I opened up the letter and read it. The words were very aggressive and cut like knives. I felt so hurt and betrayed by the individual who sent it to me. After I finished reading the letter, I began writing a hate letter to send back to that person. I finished it, and God immediately spoke to me and told me to tear that letter up. He told me to rewrite that letter and say nothing but good and pleasant things and speak highly of that person. So I tore up my hate letter and wrote things exactly as God told me. A couple days later, I mailed it off. And sometime the following week, I went back to work, and that very same person came up to me with tears in their eyes and was so emotional that they could hardly speak. I knew that God had touched this person's heart, and we both made amends with each other.

I wrote this next song sometime during the 1990s. I wanted an original title that had never been used before. I prayed about the song and asked God to help me write the right setting, and God gave me the words for the song and title. It's called "Get a Grip on Salvation." These are the words:

> On a Tennessee flight I watch as we land. I talk to a lady, her Bible in hand. She gives an impression of a minister's wife as she tells of the need for the Lord in my life. Get a grip on salvation. Let the Lord take control. Hold to His promise. Make heaven your goal. God's Word is a diamond valued more than the stars. Get a grip on salvation. Be sure where you are. My luggage in hand, a taxi nearby. Where to? says the driver. Salvation! I cry. A look of confusion, he gives me a stare. I tell him the words of the lady to share. Get a grip on salvation. Let the Lord take control. Hold to His promise. Make heaven

your goal. God's Word is a diamond valued more than the stars. Get a grip on salvation. Be sure where you are. Time has gone by since I took my flight. I searched for salvation, found it one night. In prayer at an altar, a heavenly sign. The words of the lady firm in my mind. Get a grip on salvation. Let the Lord take control. Hold to His promise. Make heaven your goal. God's Word is a diamond valued more than the stars. Get a grip on salvation. Be sure where you are. Get a grip on salvation. Let the Lord take control. Hold to His promise. Make heaven your goal. God's Word is a diamond valued more than the stars. Get a grip on salvation. Be sure where you are.

I remember one Sunday several years ago I was singing at a nursing home in Baton Rouge, Louisiana. I saw a lady visiting with someone she knew. About fifteen minutes later, she got up to leave. I began singing the previously mentioned song "Get a Grip on Salvation," and no sooner did I begin to sing the words, I noticed the lady had stopped in her tracks. All I could see was her back, but then she went to sit back down. She stayed long enough to hear the remainder of that song and a few more. As she got up to leave and I was coming to a close, she came up to me and said, "I can honestly say I've been to church twice today." I could tell how much she enjoyed my song ministry. Over the years I've been to nursing homes, retirement centers, flea markets, churches, festivals, and more. I've gotten many comments of how much it has been a blessing to many people. I am so thankful God has allowed me to have a song ministry like "Songs for Jesus." I give Him all the glory!

One of my earlier songs was written sometime between the late 1990s and early 2000s. It is one of my favorites as it reminds me of exactly who I am without God. The title of it is "Too Far from Perfect." These are the words:

> I've never walked on water or changed it to wine. I can't cause the blind to see or put an end to time. God knows I'm human. He knows where I stand. I'm too far from perfect, nothing but a man. I'll never form a man from dust of the ground. Can't calm the sea with my command or make the earth go round. I can't make the moon or the stars glow tonight. I'm too far from perfect to ever think I might. Lord, I should only do what You would want me to. I'll follow Your command. There's power in Your hand! Make me into something You can use! I've never split the waters apart in the sea. I can't make a donkey talk or set a sinner free. I won't reach perfection till heaven's my home. I'm too far from perfect to make it on my own. Lord, I should only do what You would want me to. I'll follow Your command. There's power in Your hand! Make me into something You can use! I'm too far from perfect to make it on my own. Too far from perfect to make it on my own.

This next song is one that I prayed fervently about, and God gave it to me. Everywhere I went, I sang this song, and it has always been a blessing to many people. The title of it is "He's the One." These are the words:

> All the treasure in the ocean, the earth beneath my feet. Are part of God's creation, but He means more to me. For the rugged cross long ago, He was nailed to in my place. Today reminds me of His love and His amazing grace. He's the One Who formed the heavens, the One Who

calmed the seas. He's the One Who healed the lame man, the leper, and the blind. He's the One Who's soon returning, the One Who's on my mind. If my house was filled with silver, the walls were made of gold. I still would need a Savior, salvation for my soul. Who can fill that need but Jesus? The rainbow that I see. His treasure chest of promise is eternal life for me. He's the One Who formed the heavens, the One Who calmed the seas. He's the One Who healed the lame man, the leper, and the blind. He's the One Who's soon returning, the One Who's on my mind.

My family and I were going to a church in Gonzales, Louisiana, where we were currently living. The pastor of that church was going through severe trials. I went in the prayer room, and I saw that he was hurting because the trial he was going through was so severe. I played the previously mentioned song "He's the One" in hopes of maybe cheering him up. His mood improved dramatically, and he told me, "That is as beautiful of a song as I've ever heard in my lifetime." He was really blessed by that song, and he made sure I knew that.

Years ago, sometime during the early 2000s, I attended a church service in Gonzales, Louisiana, where my family and I were at the time attending. During the message the pastor of the church mentioned how we needed to walk on the devil and step on his head. As soon as he said that, I knew I instantly had the title for a new song God wanted me to write. The title of it is "Walk on the Devil." These are the words:

> I've been in revival for the second week, tempted by the devil—he's a clever creep. I got my Bible, held it by my side. He stood by the door with another lie! I walked on the devil, stepped on his head. Used the sword of the spirit like the Lord has said! He ran like a rabbit through a briar patch. That's what the devil

does when he's attacked. That's what the devil does when he's attacked. He said I was holding to an empty bag. I said, Get behind, you filthy rag. I waved my Bible like a two-edged sword! He started to run when I praised the Lord! I walked on the devil, stepped on his head. Used the sword of the spirit like the Lord has said! He ran like a rabbit through a briar patch. That's what the devil does when he's attacked. That's what the devil does when he's attacked. He'll wait at your window like a peeping Tom, to meddle in your business when all is calm. Stirring up a problem like a hornet's nest, that's when the Lord is at His best! So walk on the devil, step on his head. Use the sword of the spirit like the Lord has said! He'll run like a rabbit through a briar patch. That's what the devil does when he's attacked. That's what the devil does when he's attacked.

The following song is one of my earlier songs I've written. It has a unique message in it. The title of it is "I've Already Looked to the Back of the Book." These are the words:

The Bible is no fairy tale. Gospel is good news, where I find peace of mind. It's the way I choose. Once I read the scriptures, I knew that I was hooked. I've already looked to the back of the book. Starting at creation to Holy Ghost salvation all through Revelation in the Word of the Lord. I want to live for Jesus, take all His advice. Not live life caught up in sin, pay an awful price. I know that I'm not a liar, don't want to be a crook. I've already looked to the back of the book. Starting at creation to Holy Ghost salvation all through Revelation in the Word of the Lord. Someone may doubt the verses that a donkey talked, man survived inside a whale, lame again did walk. Had they been with Paul or Silas when that prison shook, they too would have looked to the back of the book. Had they been with Paul or Silas when that prison shook, they too would have looked to the back of the book. I've already looked to the back of the book.

Sometime in the late 1990s or early 2000s, I wrote this following song. I had a friend of mine ask me to write him a song talking about Jesus being his hero. The title of it is "Everybody's Got a Hero." These are the words:

Everybody's got a hero, someone they will follow. On a movie screen or a magazine, you find them everywhere. On billboard signs they wine and dine like there's no tomorrow. Everybody's hero is somewhere in their life. Everybody's got a hero, but I'm so glad that I know the greatest One. Look what He's done to ease my pain and sorrow. My life has changed. I've been redeemed. I don't fear tomorrow. Everybody's hero is somewhere in their life. For on a rugged cross my hero paid the price for me. So I have life eternally, be what I can be! Everybody's got a hero, someone who builds their ego. On their shirt or socks or a breakfast box, even on some logo. But God's by far the superstar. He made the world from zero! There's no greater hero than Jesus in my life! For on a rugged cross my hero paid the price for me. So I have life eternally, be what I can be! Everybody's got a hero, someone who builds their ego. On their shirt or socks or a breakfast box, even on some logo. But God's by far the superstar. He made the world from zero! There's no greater hero than Jesus in my life! I thank the greatest hero Who's been in my life!

I remember I had a singing in Baton Rouge, Louisiana, a couple days before Christmas. This was between 1997 and 2008. As I entered into the building with my music equipment, I noticed a lady who looked very depressed sitting alone in a chair. I let her do most of the talking at first. She told me she had wanted to commit suicide throughout the week. I told her that God created her in His image and His greatest wish was that she prosper and be in health even as her soul prospered. I prayed that God would bless her and fill her with His spirit. Then I played a couple songs on my guitar that God gave me. She appreciated that so much. Then we went to another room nearby where other people were waiting for me to arrive. What could have been a depressing night instead turned into a joyful evening for all who gathered there in that room. I will never forget it on my journey to Jesus, which leads me to my next song called "He's an Awesome God."

Did you ever hear or read within the Word of God? How Jesus walked upon and calmed the stormy sea that day? Disciples feared until the wind and waves were still. What He did then He'll do again, so everyone can tell. He's an awesome God, still doing many miracles! The greatest one was done at Calvary! From the grave He rose up high to glory! To save a dying world from sin, what victory! He's an awesome God, an awesome, awesome God! Jesus multiplied the fishes and the loaves of bread. He fed five thousand souls till none were hungry, more were blessed! With clay God healed the blind. A wedding needed wine! Filled waterpots up to the brim! The best was right on time! From an awesome God, still doing many miracles! The greatest one was done at Calvary! From the grave He rose up high to glory! To save a dying world from sin, what victory! He's an awesome God, an awesome, awesome God! Devils left a man to go into a herd of swine! The man possessed could finally rest; he knew it was divine! God robed Himself in flesh

> that man was greatly blessed! When he came face-to-face that day, before an awesome God! An awesome God, still doing many miracles! The greatest one was done at Calvary! From the grave He rose up high to glory! To save a dying world from sin, what victory! He's an awesome God, an awesome, awesome God! He's an awesome God, an awesome, awesome God!

The following passage of Scripture talks about how the previously mentioned possessed man really did meet the God of glory face-to-face. 1 Timothy 3:16 says, "And without controversy, great is the mystery of godliness: God was manifest in the flesh, justified in the Spirit, seen of angels, preached unto the Gentiles, believed on in the world, received up into glory." While we were living in Gonzales, LA the pastor of the church we attended preached a message and spoke the words 'God's got a plan'. His message inspired me to write the following song. I titled it, 'God's Got a Plan.'

> God's got a plan, the Bible in His hand. A course of action suited best for me. A worker in His field, I'm part of something real. A member of God's royal family. God's got a plan that's so much better than a sinner stumbling in his misery. I found a better life through spiritual advice. I'm following the road from Calvary. My mission is divine, heavenly designed. The road is rough at times, but I'm glad. God's got a plan He didn't build on sand. He used it in that mansion built for me. Salvation for the floor, Jesus is the door. No other plan can set a sinner free. Salvation for the floor, Jesus is the door. No other plan can set a sinner free. No other plan can set a sinner free.

There are many times in my life when God has blessed me in many ways. I thank Him for that. I've learned to trust in Him more and lean not on my own understanding on my journey to Jesus. My next song called "When God Is on the Scene" explains it all. These are the words:

> The moon and stars are out tonight, a Bible in my reach. I lie in bed and think back when the Lord had pardoned me. My soul was stained like withered leaves that brushed my windowpane. Because of sin I turned to Him. God was on the scene. When God is on the scene, lives forever change. Nothing can compare to when God is on the scene. My blinded eyes were opened wide. I felt like in a dream. I floated on a cloud that day. I know God heals the lame. My miracle I waited for like flowers needing rain. I claimed it when I turned to Him. God was on the scene. He's the God of awesome power though storms will come our way. There will be a change when we call His name. God is on the scene. When God is on the scene, lives forever change. Nothing can compare to when God is on the scene. Nothing can compare to when God is on the scene.

On my journey to Jesus after obeying God's plan of salvation in Acts 2:38–39, many inspiring scriptures have blessed me greatly throughout the years. I will share them with you. Here are a few of them:

Ephesians 2:8 says, "For by grace are ye saved through faith; and that not of yourselves; it is the gift of God." 1 Corinthians 2:9 says, "But as it is written, eye has not seen, nor ear heard, neither have entered into the heart of man, the things which God has prepared for them that love him." Romans 8:28 says, "And we know that all things work together for the good to them that love God, to them who are the called according to his purpose."

Matthew 5:9 says, "Blessed are the peacemakers: for they shall be called the children of God." Matthew 5:16 says, "Let your light so shine before men, that they may see your good works, and glorify your Father which is in heaven." Psalm 139:17–18 says, "How precious also are thy thoughts unto me, O God! How great is the sum of them! If I should count them, they are more in number than the sand: when I awake, I am still with thee." Psalm 33:12 says, "Blessed is the nation whose God is the Lord, and the people he hath chosen for his own inheritance." Proverbs 3:5–6 says, "Trust in the Lord with all thine heart. Lean not on thine own understanding. In all thy ways acknowledge Him and He shall direct thy paths." Jeremiah 29:11–13 says, "For I know the thoughts that I think towards you, saith the Lord, thoughts of peace, and not of evil, to give you an expected end. Then shall ye call upon me, and I will hearken unto you. And ye shall seek me, and find me, when ye shall search for me with all your heart."

As I bring my book to a close, I just wanted to take a minute and thank my daughter McKinsey for taking the time to help and critique everything for me. She was an extremely big help to me. Lastly and most importantly, I just want to take a moment and thank my Creator for all the trials and tribulations I've gone through. They've made me into a better person while on my journey to Jesus.

After finishing high school, I became very interested in learning to play the guitar and writing songs. God gave me a dream that inspired me to read and study my Bible. "Do It All for Jesus" was the Christian song God blessed me with that led me to a music school in the New Orleans, Louisiana, area to study music theory and ear training. About six months later, I was invited to a spirit-filled church on the west bank of New Orleans, Louisiana. The Bible says that we are overcomers by the power of our testimonies.

There were times I went to visit elderly people in my neighborhood and talk to them about the Bible and God's plan for all of us. Sometimes I would bring my guitar and sing the first Christian song that God gave me called "Do It All for Jesus." Other places I've visited I handed out Bible tracts and prayed with people for their health and God's blessing upon them. I visited people in nursing homes, hospitals, and retirement centers for years. For years I had a song ministry that blessed hundreds of people in various locations across the state of Louisiana. I named the song ministry "Songs for Jesus." What happened next changed my life forever on my journey to Jesus.

The greatest blessing in my life has been my journey to Jesus. It has greatly built my faith, hope, courage, understanding, and will to please God in all my ways. Romans 8:28 says, "And we know that all things work together for the good to them that love God, to them that are the called according to His purpose." The trials and tribulations that I've been through have been many, but the blessings from God have been more. God has pulled me out of situations where I have been on the brink of death several times. Some or all those times He sent angels to protect me. Many times in prayer, I asked God to help me help myself so I can help others. He's given me the gift of faith and healing as a result. "But as it is written, Eye has not seen nor ear heard, the things which God hath prepared for them that love Him" (1 Corinthians 2:9). This book I have written, *Journey to Jesus*, is to inspire and encourage others in the ways of the Lord. Should I blame Him for sending the hail in the rain? Or placing the thorns with the roses? He is hope in the valley when I'm at my end. He's more than a man. I find no fault in Him.

On my journey to Jesus, I woke up one morning to quickly write down the words of a song that God gave me in a dream. The first verse and chorus says, "There's a better day ahead, a better world we'll see. People everywhere are friends. There's peace and harmony. Someday, someday very soon, no pain, no tears. No trouble or fears. For the children of the King, when Jesus comes again, someday very soon." The other two verses to this song are in this book.

About the Author

After finishing high school, I became very interested in learning to play the guitar and writing songs. God gave me a dream that inspired me to read and study my Bible. "Do It All For Jesus" was the Christian song God blessed me with that lead me to a music school in the New Orleans, La area to study music theory and ear training. About six months later I was invited to a spirit filled church on the west bank of New Orleans, La. The Bible says that we are overcomers by the power of our testimonies.

There were times I went visit elderly people in my neighborhood and talk to them about The Bible and God's plan for all of us. Sometimes I would bring my guitar and sing the first Christian song that God gave me called "Do It All For Jesus". Other places I've visited I handed out Bible tracts and prayed with people for their health and God's blessing upon them. I visited people in nursing homes, hospitals, and retirement centers for years. For years I had a song ministry that blessed hundreds of people in various locations across the state of Louisiana. I named the song ministry "Songs For Jesus". What happened next changed my life forever on my journey to Jesus.

CPSIA information can be obtained
at www.ICGtesting.com
Printed in the USA
LVHW041259190323
741950LV00002B/296